COLT McCOY
MATT CARTER

THE
REAL
WIN

Pursuing God's Plan for Authentic Success
GUYS BIBLE STUDY

LifeWay Press®
Nashville, Tennessee

Published by LifeWay Press®
© 2013 Colt McCoy and Matt Carter
Published by arrangement with The Waterbrook Multnomah
Publishing Group, a division of Random House Inc.

ISBN 978-1-4300-3263-2
Item 005648011

DEWEY: 248.834
SUBHD: STUDENTS \ SUCCESS \ CHRISTIAN LIFE

To order additional copies of this resource, write to LifeWay Church Resources
Customer Service; One LifeWay Plaza; Nashville, TN 37234-0113; fax
615.251.5933; phone toll free 800.458.2772; order online at www.lifeway.com; email
orderentry@lifeway.com; or visit the LifeWay Christian Store serving you.

Printed in the United States of America.

Student Ministry Publishing
LifeWay Church Resources
One LifeWay Plaza
Nashville, TN 37234-0144

CONTENTS

THE **AUTHORS**

COLT McCOY is an NFL quarterback. As a college player at the University of Texas, he was the most winning quarterback in the history of NCAA football, leading the Longhorns to the 2010 BCS National Championship game. During his senior year Colt won 13 of the top 15 major college-player awards, including quarterback of the year, offensive player of the year, and outstanding football player of the year. He was also a 2008 Heisman trophy runner-up. Colt has been involved in domestic and international ministries. He and his wife, Rachel, live in Austin, Texas. For more information visit *www.coltmccoy.com.*

MATT CARTER serves as the pastor of preaching and vision at Austin Stone Community Church in Austin, Texas. Planted in 2002, the church has grown from a core team of 15 to more than 8,000 regular attendees today. Matt holds a master's degree in divinity from Southwestern Seminary and is pursuing a doctorate of ministry from Southeastern Seminary. He is a coauthor of *For the City* and of the LifeWay Bible studies *Creation Unraveled* and *Creation Restored.* Matt and his wife, Jennifer, live in Austin with their three children. For more information visit *www.austinstone.org.*

INTRODUCTION

If you're like most guys, you want to win. You pursue success and hate losing. Winning is described as, "The taste of victory," and losing is described as "the sting of defeat." We all want something that tastes good, especially when the other option is a sting. The question we need to ask then is this, "What are we doing in our lives that sets us up for victory?" If success is what we want, and we all do, then how do we really achieve it?

That's why we've written this study—because we've discovered there's a real win out there for each of us. There's a real win out there for you. There's a way to live and love and work and play that feels genuine instead of hollow. And it's a way that allows us to become the men we were truly created to be.

We don't promise that everything will be rosy, because it won't. You'll still fail, as we did. You'll have to learn some things the hard way, as we still do. But we can promise the teaching in this study is based on biblical principles and the more you learn to pursue God's way of doing things, the more your definition of *success* will change and grow in the most important areas of your life. In other words, your quest for authentic success can start here. We call it the real win.

Over the next 7 weeks, we are going to take you along on a few hunts we went on this year. Along the way we are going to have some conversations that we feel God will use to help you understand His plan and your role in that plan.

HERE'S WHAT WE ARE ASKING FROM YOU:
1. **Commit to reading each week.** Spend 10 minutes a day studying with us.
2. **Write down your answers.** You have to put some pen to paper and think through these questions.
3. **Share with your group.** This is a process for all us, none of us have arrived yet. Speak up and don't be afraid to face your failures or weaknesses.
4. **Pray.** Pray each day that God would open your eyes to the areas in your life preventing you from the real win. Allow Him to move you into a place where you trust Him and follow where He leads.

It's that simple. Join us as we seek the real win.

THE REAL WIN

WHAT IS **SUCCESS**?

When it comes to the game of life, many of us are aiming at different targets. We have many different definitions of what it means to be successful in this world.

For example, success might be...
- becoming the starting QB;
- dating the best-looking girl in school;
- throwing the biggest party of the year;
- getting straight A's;
- being the most popular guy in school;
- being respected by others;
- leaving a legacy at your school.

These examples of success reflect the most popular values in our culture; they surround us every day. Do you see the ultimate goal of your life represented in the list? Or are you aiming at a different target as you live and work each day—a different purpose?

We'll begin this study by redefining *success* in a way that's significantly different from the previous examples; we'll look at success from God's perspective. In doing so, we'll gain a better understanding of what it means to serve God faithfully and to trust Him with our lives. And through it all, we'll start to discover what the real win is all about.

Write your definition of *success* below.

WRESTLING WITH SUCCESS

COLT'S STORY

My whole life I've been hardwired to win. My dad was a successful coach for more than 25 years, so I learned early on that there's a pretty fine line between winning and losing, success and failure. I also learned early on that I don't like to lose.

Now if you're a boy growing up in Texas with a football in your hands, chances are good that you dream of playing at the University of Texas, leading your team to victory during the national championship, and winning the Heisman Trophy to be recognized as the best college football player in the country. That WAS the ultimate victory for me.

I came so close.

During my senior year in 2009 I was the starting quarterback for the University of Texas Longhorns. We had a great team, and we'd had a great season by the time I traveled to New York City for the presentation of the Heisman Trophy. This was my second year as a finalist for the award, and I felt that I had a good chance to win. In the closest points race since 1985, I came in third. Not bad, but the bottom line was that I didn't win. Part of my chance for ultimate victory was gone.

Still, we had the National Championship to play for—another chance to accomplish the dream I'd been pushing for my whole life. We were the underdogs against the University of Alabama Crimson Tide, but I was confident we could win. I'd played with my teammates for four years at that point, and I knew what we were capable of.

I came across Isaiah 26:3-4 during my devotions in the days leading up to the National Championship:

> You keep him in perfect peace
> whose mind is stayed on you,
> because he trusts in you.
> Trust in the LORD forever,
> for the LORD GOD is an everlasting rock.

That's the text I meditated on as I took the field for the biggest game of my life, and it's become the passage that undergirds what my life is about today.

The game itself couldn't have started out much better for my team and me. Our defense intercepted the ball from Alabama, and our offense drove right down the field. I completed several passes in a row and was trying to run for a score when I got hit by a three-hundred-pound defensive lineman and felt something go wrong with my right shoulder—my throwing shoulder.

It wasn't a huge hit. I'd taken a lot worse over the years, and I wanted to bounce right up and try again for that touchdown. But my right arm was numb from the shoulder to my fingers; I couldn't raise it or grip the ball. I was in shock as I jogged over to the sideline and talked with our trainers. I wanted to get back on the field!

But I never did. The trainers worked to get me back in shape while my backup, a freshman, did his best to lead our offense. Eventually, I was taken to the locker room to confirm the worst: my arm wasn't getting better anytime soon. I sat on the bench for the rest of the game and watched as my team fought valiantly. In the end, though, we lost.

My dream was dead.

Walking off the field after the game, I felt more disappointed than at any other point in my life. That's when the sideline reporter for ABC News tugged on my jersey and asked for an interview. I nodded, and she asked the question I knew was coming: "Colt, what was it like for you to watch this game—the last game in uniform—from the sideline?"

I didn't know what to say, so I started by talking about my passion for the game of football and about how much I wanted to get back on the field. I congratulated Alabama on its victory and praised my team for fighting hard.

Then I said something that still surprises me to this day: "I always give God the glory. I never question why things happen the way they do. God is in control of my life, and I know that if nothing else, I'm standing on the Rock."

I know those words came to me because of God. Yes, they came partly because I'd been meditating on Isaiah 26:3-4 before the game, but there was more to it. During the most difficult and disappointing moment of my life, God gave me peace.

Something clicked into place, and I truly understood that God was my Rock and that my life wouldn't be shattered, no matter how many dreams I failed to achieve.

I realized that God was in control, and He would always be in control.

What are some of your most ambitious dreams? Record three.
1.

2.

3.

How will you view your life if you look back and none of those dreams came true? What if they all do?

Look again at Isaiah 26:3-4. What does it mean that God is "an everlasting rock" (v. 4)?

REDEFINING *SUCCESS*

One of the nice things about sports is that it's pretty easy to figure out whether you're winning or losing. If you're playing football and your team has more points than the other team, you're winning. If you're running a race and you see someone running in front of you, you're losing. It's simple.

Unfortunately, real life is more complicated. Most guys like to win as often as possible, but when it comes to everyday life, there are no specific measures that tell us whether we're ahead of the game or behind. There isn't a scorecard that works for us all.

Take a few minutes and think through what success would look like in your life right now. Just list a couple of situations you face on a daily basis and then write down what a win in that situation would look like. An example would be:

- **Getting better grades. A win would look like me doing more work and not copying my friend's work.**

-

-

-

-

-

-

Here's the point: we all define *success* in different ways. We all have dreams we're shooting for and goals we're trying to achieve. But are they the right dreams? Are they the correct goals? Is what we are doing everyday pushing us closer to success or further from it? How can anyone know?

We've written this study because both of us have tried to come up with our own versions of success in this life, and we've both failed. You'll hear more about those failures—and the lessons we learned from them—in the pages to come. Thankfully, all of the times we've missed the mark have helped us gain a better understanding of what authentic success looks like for guys who are attempting to follow Christ.

Go beyond writing a definition for success. Make it personal. Success for me would look like:

How confident are you that you're winning in the game of your life?

What makes you think that way?

The concept of the real win is built on two simple but strategic components: whom you serve and whom you trust. Those two decisions change everything, and we'll take a deeper look at each one this week.

What we need you to understand now is that pursuing the real win may require you to redefine your definition of *success*. It may require you to change your understanding of what it means to win by exploring what success looks like through the lens of the Bible rather than through the lenses of our culture, or your own desires.

Are you willing to do that? Pursuing the real win takes resolve, and the decision to shoot for it is a choice you make more than once. It requires courage, faith, and determination—and it certainly isn't always easy.

But take it from two guys who've been knocked down a few times and learned a few things: it's worth it.

WHY FAITHFULNESS IS KEY

The real win in this life is built on two simple ideas:
- whom you serve
- whom you trust

You've probably figured out that God should be the *whom* in both of those phrases. People can find authentic success in life only when they commit to serve God and trust Him. What does that actually mean for guys like us? It is one thing to talk about it, but what does it look like to serve God every day? Why should we trust Him, and how do we go about it?

What ideas or images come to mind when you think of serving God?

What does trusting God mean to you?

Let's start by taking a deeper look at what it means for us to serve God as we search for the real win.

FAITHFUL IN SMALL THINGS

In the Bible, a good place to start exploring the concept of serving God is Jesus' parable of the talents in Matthew 25. If you're not familiar with that story, a rich guy went on a long journey. Before he left, he gave different sums of money to three of his servants in order to keep his business rolling. The first guy got five talents, the second guy got two talents, and the third guy got one talent. A talent was payment for six thousand days of work, so each servant received a lot of money. The first two servants immediately got to work and started investing the money they'd been given. But the third servant took a different approach. He decided to hide the money by digging a hole and burying it.

Here's what happened next:

> Now after a long time the master of those servants came and settled accounts with them. And he who had received the five talents came forward, bringing five talents more, saying, "Master, you delivered to me five talents; here I have made five talents more." His master said to him, "Well done, good and faithful servant. You have been faithful over a little; I will set you over much. Enter into the joy of your master."
> **MATTHEW 25:19-21**

Notice that the word *faithful* pops up a couple times. That's an important concept to keep in mind when it comes to serving God. Here's the dictionary definition:
Faithful: *(1) strict or thorough in the performance of duty: a faithful worker; (2) true to one's word, promises, vows, etc.; (3) steady in allegiance or affection; loyal; constant.*[1]

Would friends and family members describe you as faithful? Why?

The second servant got the same praise as the first one. But the third didn't fare so well. He dug up the talent he'd been given, wiped off the dirt, and brought it back. He said he'd been afraid because the master was a "hard man" (v. 24), and he didn't want to risk losing anything. So he'd done nothing with the money. Not surprisingly, the master wasn't impressed:

> But his master answered him, "You wicked and slothful servant! You knew that I reap where I have not sown and gather where I scattered no seed? Then you ought to have invested my money with the bankers, and at my coming I should have received what was my own with interest. So take the talent from him and give it to him who has the ten talents. For to everyone who has will more be given, and he will have an abundance. But from the one who has not, even what he has will be taken away. And cast the worthless servant into the outer darkness. In that place there will be weeping and gnashing of teeth."
> **MATTHEW 25:26-30**

What's the difference between the first two servants and the third servant? Faithfulness. The first two servants had been given resources, and they faithfully served their master by using those resources to do the work their master wanted done. The third servant focused on himself rather than his master. He didn't want to work; he didn't want to take risks. So he did nothing. He was unfaithful.

Here's the point: authentic success in this life means being faithful with the little things God gives us. The servants were not rewarded for their success or accomplishments. They were simply faithful and did what the master asked of them. We find the real win by serving God and doing His work with whatever resources we've got.

What are some of the main resources you've been given that could be used to serve God and do His work on earth?

Which of these resources are being wasted on pursuits that don't have eternal significance?

What steps could you take this week to make better use of one or two of those resources?

We'll keep digging into this concept as we move through the study and focus on key pursuits such as leadership, work, family, and so on. For now, though, notice how the first two servants were rewarded. When they faithfully served with a few resources, they were given more resources—not to get lazy and happy with, but to continue serving and doing their master's work on a larger scale.

The same can be true of us. When we're faithful to serve God with whatever He's given us, He will give us greater opportunities to serve faithfully and do the work of His kingdom.

FAITHFUL AT ALL TIMES

We just talked about the good news: we can experience the real win as guys by faithfully serving God with the little things He gives us. And as we're faithful in those small things, He will give us a chance to be faithful with bigger things. That's authentic success.

Now here's the bad news: it won't be smooth sailing for any of us. We'll all go through tough times and difficult circumstances—even if we're serving God. If you don't agree, just look at these words from the apostle Paul:

> Five times I received at the hands of the Jews the forty lashes less one. Three times I was beaten with rods. Once I was stoned. Three times I was shipwrecked; a night and a day I was adrift at sea; on frequent journeys, in danger from rivers, danger from robbers, danger from my own people, danger from Gentiles, danger in the city, danger in the wilderness, danger at sea, danger from false brothers; in toil and hardship, through many a sleepless night, in hunger and thirst, often without food, in cold and exposure.
> **2 CORINTHIANS 11:24-27**

Paul was describing just some of the hardships he'd been through in his efforts to serve God and spread the gospel message. Even as he was serving God faithfully, he still faced all kinds of adversity. The same will be true for us.

How have you experienced tough times in the past year?

How did those tough times affect the way you used your resources in serving God?

The big challenge for us is to continue faithfully serving God even when things get tough. We need to keep working and keep the right focus even when challenges knock us down, even when we feel disappointed or discouraged, and even when we don't understand what's going on. We need to remember God is not holding us accountable for the results, but rather how faithfully we served.

What helps you stay focused on a challenging task?

How can you stay focused on God during a challenging time?

When we serve God and are faithful with the little things, despite the troubles in our lives, we'll hear the same words the first two servants heard:

> "Well done, good and faithful servant. You have been faithful over a little; I will set you over much. Enter into the joy of your master."
> **MATTHEW 25:23**

We'll be able to say what Paul said near the end of his life:

> I have fought the good fight, I have finished the race, I have kept the faith. Henceforth there is laid up for me the crown of righteousness, which the Lord, the righteous judge, will award to me on that Day, and not only to me but also to all who have loved his appearing.
> **2 TIMOTHY 4:7-8**

That's the real win.

FAITHFULNESS AND YOU

MATT'S STORY

I have vivid memories of the night I began to feel massive pains in the pit of my stomach, completely out of the blue. I was taken to the hospital and was told I needed an emergency appendectomy. The operation went well. I stayed overnight to be safe, and then I went home. Problem solved.

Or so I thought. A couple days later I was sitting at my desk at work when I got a phone call from my wife. She'd heard from the doctor. They'd found a malignant tumor in my appendix after the operation. I had cancer.

It turned out to be a carcinoid tumor of the appendix, which is a fairly rare type of cancer. Such tumors typically start to spread either when they become 2.0 centimeters long or when they break through the appendix wall. My tumor was 1.9 centimeters long and had already broken through the wall, so this was bad.

Doctors also told me that if this type of cancer spreads into your lymph nodes, you're done. Chemo doesn't work. Radiation doesn't work. It's a slow-growing cancer, so it takes a few years to kill you. And there's no hope.

I'll spare you the gory details of all my tests, but the result was that my blood levels came back abnormally high, and my lymph nodes had swollen significantly—a double dose of bad news. It looked as if the cancer had already spread. The other possibility was that my blood markers were high because of the original tumor and that my lymph nodes were swollen because of the surgery. The only way to know for sure was to wait a few months and see whether anything changed, but I could tell the doctors were less than hopeful. Chances were slim that it would turn out all right.

As a 31-year-old man, I was preparing to die.

For the next three months I sat on pins and needles, thinking, hoping, and praying. I experienced every dark emotion imaginable. What would happen to my wife and children? What would happen to my church? I struggled to understand why God would allow this to happen to me.

During the darkest of those days, a friend pointed me to Psalm 39:4-5. He'd been praying for me, and he felt that God wanted to speak to me through that passage:

> "Show me, O LORD, my life's end
> and the number of my days;
> let me know how fleeting is my life.
> You have made my days a mere handbreadth;
> the span of my years is as nothing before you.
> Each man's life is but a breath." (NIV)

I chewed on those verses awhile. Have you ever breathed on a window on a cold winter's day? It fogs up, but then the fog instantly disappears. That's what David was saying a man's life is like—here for a brief moment, then gone. David knew that when a man grasps how short his life is, he begins to live with a new sense of what's truly important.

God was showing me there's a direct connection between understanding how short my life is and the urgency with which I'd live that life. God wanted to teach me how to number my days, how to know time was short, and how not to live in vain. God wanted me to live with holy urgency. That was a tough lesson to learn, and I was still missing an essential ingredient: *trust*.

The night before my next round of tests—the ones that would tell me whether I'd live or die—I paced around my bedroom and vented to my wife, Jennifer, about how frustrated I felt. Anxious and exhausted, I yelled, "What does God want from me? I've done everything I can think of. What's He trying to teach me?" Calmly, my wife looked at me and said, "Matt, I don't know what God's trying to teach you. But I know this: He wants you to *trust Him.*"

The next day I went to the cancer ward and sat in the waiting room, surrounded by dying people. My Bible in my hands, I began reading the account of Jesus on the cross. As I read, I realized that Jesus fully trusted God even while He was being tortured and crucified. The cross didn't look like a win for someone who was going to save the world. Yet the cross was exactly what God had planned for Jesus. The nails were in Jesus' hands for a reason.

Something turned in my heart, and it hit me like a bolt of lightning: sometimes trusting God means you don't get to climb down from your cross.

Whatever difficulty you're bearing, whatever goal you're not achieving, staying in that difficulty might be a part of God's perfect plan for your life. In other words, losing in the eyes of the world might be success in the eyes of God.

After my second round of tests, I went back to my office, got on my knees, and prayed, "Lord, if it's Your will for me to die, I trust You." I'd said this to Him before, but this was the first time I really meant it. I fully surrendered right then. I let go. A peace and confidence came over me as I'd never felt before. Without a shadow of a doubt, I knew that every moment of my life was in God's hands.

The next day a phone call came. My blood work was normal. My lymph nodes were normal. All of my test results were normal. There was no sign of cancer anywhere! As of the writing of this book, I've been completely cancer-free for seven years. Now I don't know if God miraculously healed me, or if I'd never had any other cancer besides the appendix tumor. And I'm not saying that if you trust God, He will solve your problems the way my cancer was taken away from me. But this is what I know for sure: God brought me to a place where I said, "If You want to keep me on the cross, then I trust You." And I still do.

Who are some people you trust most in this life? Why do you trust them?

How well do you trust God with the circumstances in your life?

CHOOSE TO TRUST

We've made the case that authentic success isn't about big achievements and flashy victories in this life. Rather, the real win means faithfully serving God in the little things, especially when the going gets tough. But how? How can we stay faithful and keep serving when we feel beaten down or afraid—when we don't even understand what God wants from us?

The answer is trust. You can't serve God—you can't be faithful with the resources He's given you—unless you trust Him.

1. "Faithful," *Dictionary.com* [online, cited 1 April 2013]. Available from the Internet: *http://dictionary.reference.com.*

LEADERSHIP

YOU ARE A **LEADER**

There are many leaders in today's society, and there are just as many different titles and descriptions we use to label leaders. Here are just a few: coach, boss, president, parent, manager, captain, and so on.

Do you wear one of those labels? Do you have dreams to wear one someday? Leadership isn't something that is reserved for adulthood. Right where you are, there is need for leadership. There's also another leadership label we need to add to the list above: *man*. While you may never hold an official position that places you in leadership over other people, you will inevitably one day be a man.

That's right. If you're a guy, you're called to lead. One day as a husband you'll be called to lead your wife. One day as a father you'll be called to lead your children. If you have a job, live in a community, or attend a church, you'll be called to be a witness for God's kingdom and lead within those areas of influence.

Does that mean women shouldn't be leaders or aren't qualified to have positions of influence in today's culture? No, we're not saying that. Women can be gifted leaders too. But as we'll see this week, the Bible makes it clear that *all* men are called to lead. All men are leaders, so it's important for all men to understand what leadership means and how they can fulfill their roles in God's kingdom.

CALLED TO LEAD

COLT'S STORY

I know what it's like to lead. I also know what it's like to struggle with the weight and responsibility of leadership. As a quarterback, I strive to be a leader on my team both on and off the field. That's a skill I've cultivated over the years—in high school, in college, and now in the NFL. I strive to set a high standard for myself, and I ask my teammates to follow.

But things are a little different for me as a new husband. I'm still learning my responsibilities in that arena—what I'm supposed to do, what I can do, and what I should never do. I've found it can be harder to lead a marriage than an NFL team!

In my first season with the Cleveland Browns, Matt and Jennifer came to visit my wife, Rachel, and me. I was going through a rough patch in my job. We were playing well as a football team, but we were still losing. Matt and Jenn came to our game against the St. Louis Rams. In the last few minutes of the game, our team drove the ball all the way downfield to set up a game-winning field goal. But because of a rare misplaced snap, our kicker missed the field goal, and we lost.

Later that night I was feeling pretty low as the four of us talked together. I kept asking whether it was all worth it—the punishment, pain, and scrutiny of being in the spotlight all the time. Rachel confessed to Matt and Jenn how hard it was to see me depressed like that. It's not easy for a young wife to see her husband so down, and this wasn't the first time I'd been this way. My attitude was difficult on our marriage, the stress was taking a toll, and we were finding it difficult to connect with each other in the midst of it all. I've since learned that difficult circumstances are the exact times when a man needs to lead.

Recently, Matt and Jenn came back for another visit, this time in the summer. I'd done some good thinking and praying since the last time they'd seen us, but my job was still difficult. In fact, the Browns had drafted another quarterback only a few months earlier, and I was working hard to keep my job as a starter. Because of the hours I was putting into training, I wasn't doing a great job of communicating well with the people I loved.

Matt and Jenn were worried, so they came to see us. One evening while I was still at the training facility, Jenn asked my wife, "How is Colt doing? And be honest."

Rachel said, "Honestly, it's been great. Colt's been a different man this year compared to what was happening inside him last year. His job is still incredibly stressful, but he's changing as a man and husband. Now he comes home and makes a conscious effort to be present. The only thing I can figure out is that God has done a good work in his heart."

She was right. I'd been spending a lot of time with God, and He'd been helping me redefine my views of success. I had a better understanding of what was important and what wasn't, and I was learning to be faithful in serving Him (and the people closest to me) even when things were disappointing with my job.

Matt later told me how happy he was to hear about those changes. He could see that God was working on my heart and that I was responding to His call for me to lead well at home. I was learning to live not as an immature guy, but as a mature man seeking authentic success.

Again, the change wasn't due to anything special in me. It was all thanks to God's work in my life.

What ideas or images come to mind when you hear the word *leader*?

Who among your friends and family do you consider a good leader? Record three examples and include what attributes help each person lead well.
1.

2.

3.

When have you recently been asked to lead in a specific area?

What happened?

BORN LEADERS

A TV sitcom featured an episode in which a teenage girl and her boyfriend discovered they were going to have a baby. Naturally, they were both scared and unsure of what to do. One scene showed the young man losing his cool, which didn't help matters. The girl needed the guy to stay calm and commit to see the situation through.

Finally, in an outburst of anger, the girl looked at him and said, "Somewhere inside of that pea-brain of yours is a man. Access him!"[1]

Let's face it: there are lots of guys out there who don't consider themselves to be leaders. You may be one of them. You may not feel prepared or capable of handling the reins in a difficult situation.

How confident are you in your ability to lead?

What are you doing in your life to help you be able to lead better?

No matter how you feel, the Scriptures are clear that God has specifically called guys to lead. It started way back in the garden of Eden:

> God said, "Let us make man in our image, after our likeness. And let them have dominion over the fish of the sea and over the birds of the heavens and over the livestock and over all the earth and over every creeping thing that creeps on the earth." So God created man in his own image, in the image of God he created him; male and female he created them. And God blessed them. And God said to them, "Be fruitful and multiply and fill the earth and subdue it, and have dominion over the fish of the sea and over the birds of the heavens and over every living thing that moves on the earth."
> **GENESIS 1:26-28**

What's your initial reaction to these verses?

How do you understand the word *rule* in the context of these verses?

From the earliest moments of creation, men receive a leadership role in this world. We're stewards over creation, so we have a responsibility to care for the world around us. Of course, no individual can care for the entire world, so we all have a responsibility to ensure that God's will is carried out in our specific spheres of influence.

Several Scripture passages make it clear that men bear a larger portion of that responsibility than women. Look at 1 Corinthians 11:3, for example:

> But I want you to understand that the head of every man is Christ,
> the head of a wife is her husband, and the head of Christ is God.

That doesn't mean men are more important than women, better than women, or more valuable than women. It just means men are called to carry out a specific role as leaders within their spheres of influence.

Living in today's culture—and specifically as guys seeking to follow God and do His work—we're not to be passive. We're not to shift our responsibilities onto others. The Bible teaches that we're to take the lead in our dating relationships, teams, churches, communities, and families.

We're called to be leaders.

THE DESTRUCTIVE POWER OF BAD LEADERS

In most sports it's pretty easy to identify when people fail to perform their roles. If an offensive lineman fails to block a hard-charging defensive end, for example, his quarterback is going to get hammered. If a power forward on an NBA team doesn't play defense, someone on the other team is going to wind up on *SportsCenter* with a spectacular dunk.

It's often more difficult to pinpoint the sources of failure in the real world. For example, who should receive the blame for the following situations?

- Your team is on a four game losing streak.
- Your girlfriend is pregnant.
- You failed your last test.
- Your parents are getting a divorce.
- You experience significant conflict with a family member or a friend.

How have you handled any of the previous situations?

Are you struggling with one right now? What should you do to improve the situation?

How do you typically react when you fail to do something well?

While we are called to lead, that doesn't mean it will be simple for us, or that we all will do a good job of leading. Not by a long shot. Unfortunately that doesn't give us an out. Just like in sports, when things aren't going well, you figure out why and you create a game plan to address the weakness. Although the source of our failures isn't always obvious, the consequences of failing to lead well are clearly evident.

A BAD START

Here's a sobering thought: the first man ever created was also the first man to demonstrate poor leadership in a critical situation. We're talking about Adam, of course.

Yes, it was Eve who ate the forbidden fruit and ultimately committed the first sin, but we need to ask an important question about that world-changing event: Where was Adam when all the bad stuff went down?

Scriptures gives us the answer:

> When the woman saw that the tree was good for food, and that
> it was a delight to the eyes, and that the tree was to be desired to
> make one wise, she took of its fruit and ate, and she
> also gave some to her husband who was with her, and he ate.
> **GENESIS 3:6**

What's your initial reaction to this verse?

How does this verse reflect on Adam's role as a leader?

Let's be clear: Adam was *right there* when sin entered the world. God created him to rule in the garden—to lead, to take action when necessary. Yet he did nothing. When his wife disobeyed God's command, Adam just stood there with his hands in his pockets like a chump. (Metaphorically, of course. Don't forget, clothes hadn't been created yet.)

As if his passive leadership wasn't bad enough, when he finally decided to act, he joined Eve in the fruit-tasting party. He failed to lead his wife by not helping her in a time of temptation, and he failed to lead by example when he did the wrong thing in a difficult situation.

List examples from your life of passive leadership failures. These would be failures to act when you should have.

Now list times when you acted, but failed to lead correctly in that moment.

Here's the thing we need to understand as guys. Although Eve committed the first sin, the Bible makes it clear that God held Adam responsible:

> Just as sin came into the world through one man, and death through sin, and so death spread to all men because all sinned—for sin indeed was in the world before the law was given, but sin is not counted where there is no law. Yet death reigned from Adam to Moses, even over those whose sinning was not like the transgression of Adam, who was a type of the one who was to come.
> **ROMANS 5:12-14**

What were the consequences of Adam's failure to lead well?

How have you experienced these consequences in recent days?

Scripture is clear: the sinful nature of humankind and the broken nature of the world today can both be traced back to *one man* who sat on the sidelines during a critical situation. And it changed everything for the worse.

A GOLDEN MISTAKE

Adam isn't the only example in the Bible of a man who failed to lead well. In fact, the list is too long to begin writing down.

Look at Aaron, for instance. He was supposed to be Moses' right-hand man while the Israelites were heading toward the promised land after the exodus from Egypt. But when Moses went to speak with God on Mount Sinai, Aaron completely failed to lead his people well. Check out the Scripture below.

> When the people saw that Moses delayed to come down from the mountain, the people gathered themselves together to Aaron and said to him, "Up, make us gods who shall go before us. As for this Moses, the man who brought us up out of the land of Egypt, we do not know what has become of him."
> **EXODUS 32:1**

The Israelites were afraid because they hadn't seen Moses for days and there was a huge storm surrounding the mountain. This was a chance for Aaron to take charge and steer the Israelites away from their fear and idolatry—a chance for him to step up and lead.

But he blew it. Telling the people to gather their gold, Aaron made an idol for them to worship in the shape of a calf. So, instead of leading the people away from idolatry, he led them deeper into sin.

When have you been hurt or led astray because of poor leadership?

Why is fear never an excuse to abandon your role as a leader?

How do you generally respond in times of fear?

One of the more disappointing elements in this story is that Aaron wasn't even man enough to take responsibility for his failure. When Moses came charging back down the mountain and confronted him about the golden calf, Aaron blamed everyone but himself:

> Aaron said, "Let not the anger of my lord burn hot. You know the people, that they are set on evil. For they said to me, 'Make us gods who shall go before us. As for this Moses, the man who brought us up out of the land of Egypt, we do not know what has become of him.' So I said to them, 'Let any who have gold take it off.' So they gave it to me, and I threw it into the fire, and out came this calf."
> **EXODUS 32:22-24**

"It's the people's fault. They're set on evil, and they brought me all this gold. All I did was throw it in the fire, and out came a calf—like magic!"

How was Aaron's failure similar to Adam's?

Look at Genesis 3:8-13. How was Aaron's response to his failure similar to Adam's response in the garden of Eden?

There are many more examples of failed leaders in the Bible. Moses himself made several mistakes, as did guys like Samson, Saul, David, Peter, and so on. All of them caused damage because of their failures and mistakes, just as we cause damage whenever we miss the mark as leaders today. Fortunately, the Bible tells us one Man always did the right thing as a leader. We'll talk more about Him and what He can teach us as we finish up this week's study.

LEADERSHIP AND YOU

MATT'S STORY

A while back I was standing around talking with a group of people at a backyard event associated with my church when I noticed a little boy hanging around as if he didn't have anything to do. He was about 10 years old, the same age as my daughter, so I walked over to have a friendly chat. I started by asking where his dad was.

"On a business trip," the boy said. "He's going to be gone for a couple of weeks."

"Oh. Do you miss your dad when he's gone like that?"

"Nah, not really."

I was shocked. "How come?" I asked.

"Well, he's never around even when he's home," the boy said. "When he is, he's always in his office working. I only see him a few minutes each day. Honestly, he doesn't pay much attention to us."

In less than seven seconds that boy spoke a mouthful. In fact, it broke my heart. I was expecting to hear the opposite—that he missed his dad greatly. I certainly hope if I were gone on business and somebody asked my kids if they missed me, they'd say, "Absolutely."

Now I don't know this boy's father, and I don't know the specific circumstances of this family's life. Maybe the father doesn't have a choice to live differently than he's doing right now. Or maybe the boy was just having a bad day and venting about his father being gone.

Either way, though, the situation wasn't working for that family. Something was wrong, damage was being done, and it all pointed to a failure in leadership on one level or another.

What type of example is your father in regard to leadership of your family?

What are the consequences you see of his ability to lead or his inability to lead?

How well do you do as a leader within your family? How can you do a better job?

FOLLOWING THE LEADER

We started this study by exploring the need to redefine *success*—to move away from our culture's definition of a good life and instead concentrate on trusting God and serving Him. That's the real win.

We've been talking about leadership this week. Guys are created to lead within their specific spheres of influence, and in doing so, help others experience the real win as well. When we fulfill our roles as leaders, we guide our family, friends, neighbors, and teammates to experience authentic success for themselves.

Unfortunately, we don't always lead the right way. We mess up sometimes, and our failures often cause damage to the people we care most about—as in the story of the little boy and his father.

Basically, we have two conflicting ideas: (1) men are called to lead, but (2) men often fail in their attempts to lead well. How can we reconcile those two statements? How can we fulfill our roles as leaders in spite of our failures?

What's your initial reaction to the previous questions?

How does our culture typically react to the failures of those who lead?

The first thing to keep in mind is that we aren't called to perfection. Yes, we need to do our best in all situations, but James 3:2 makes it clear that "we all stumble in many ways." That certainly includes those who serve as leaders. Romans 3:23 reminds us that we "all have sinned and fall short of the glory of God." If we ignore these realities, we only makes things worse because we end up refusing to admit our failures, as Adam and Aaron did.

Do you feel pressure to avoid mistakes as a guy or as a follower of God? Explain.

How difficult is it to admit when you have made a mistake?

Does it matter who is affected by the mistake?

The solution to dealing with your failures isn't simply to try harder. You've probably been down that road, haven't you? You make a mistake, and you think, *Next time I'll do better. Next time I'll work harder or pray more, and things will be different.* But how has that worked out for you?

When have you tried to avoid mistakes by working harder? What happened?

Remember, we're broken. This brokenness isn't a little crack or dent. We're completely broken. We're sinful. We don't have the capacity to fix what's wrong with us, so we'll continue to fail no matter how hard we try to do things better next time. So, how can we function well as men whom God has called to lead? The answer is to turn to Jesus and pursue Him—to serve Him because we trust Him and we know that *He* will lead us in the right direction even when we have no idea what to do or where to go.

In other words, we've talked about redefining success, but we also need to redefine leadership. Only to the extent that we follow Jesus will we be able to lead those whom God has entrusted to us. The apostle Paul gave us a clear picture of this reality in this passage from the Book of Romans:

> If, because of one man's trespass, death reigned through that one man, much more will those who receive the abundance of grace and the free gift of righteousness reign in life through the one man Jesus Christ. Therefore, as one trespass led to condemnation for all men, so one act of righteousness leads to justification and life for all men.
> **ROMANS 5:17-18**

Do you see the logic here? Even though sin entered the world through the failures of the first man, Adam, the restoring work of Jesus Christ trumps all Adam ever did. Because Jesus perfectly fulfilled His role as a leader, we don't have to be perfect ourselves. Rather, we have "the abundance of grace and the free gift of righteousness" (v. 17). That's why Paul could say, "Follow my example, as I follow the example of Christ" (1 Cor. 11:1, NIV).

Jesus is the only Man who ever lived perfectly—the only Leader who ever fulfilled His role without any mistakes. He died on the cross, was raised in power, and now lives in us and gives us the ability to walk boldly through life and lead more and more like Him each day.

Therefore, trusting and following Jesus is the only hope we have to lead well as guys. Serving Jesus is the only way we can fulfill our roles and benefit those we care about.

How does your relationship with Jesus affect your leadership in the following areas?

- **At home:**

- **At school:**

- **In your community:**

- **In your church:**

As a man, you're called to lead. And as a human being, you're going to stumble at times in your efforts to obey that call. Thankfully, the way for us to deal with our failures as guys and as leaders is to follow Jesus. That means going where He wants us to go and doing what He wants us to do—seeking, obeying, and depending on Him rather than trying to figure everything out ourselves. That's how we live up to the call God has placed on our lives as men.

1. "Wheels," episode 9 of "Glee," originally aired November 11, 2009.

IDOLATRY

SPOTTING THE **HOOK**

The sport of fishing has become increasingly complicated in recent years. Improvements in technology mean you can spend thousands of dollars on sophisticated boats, baits, rods, depth finders, and more. You can study maps, charts, and seasons, and pour hours into determining where the biggest fish will be and what's required to catch them.

But when you get down to it, the basic idea of fishing has remained unchanged for thousands of years: you catch a fish by offering it something that looks enticing, but ultimately leaves the fish dangling on the end of your line.

Of course, the key element from a fisherman's perspective is the hook. That's what enables you to snare the fish and make it yours once it decides to take the bait.

This week we're going to look at the concept of *idolatry*. That's not a word we use often today, even in the church, and it's a concept we don't usually apply to our modern lives. But maybe we should take a fresh look at it.

Whether or not we recognize it, idolatry is present in the heart of every person. It's a deep-seated sin that diverts us from God's plan for authentic success to pursue goals and achievements that are ultimately worthless.

As we'll see in the pages to come, these false pursuits cause an incredible amount of damage to our souls. They bring wave after wave of pain and disappointment in our lives because idolatry always comes with a hook.

DEFINING IDOLATRY

MATT'S STORY

As of the writing of this study, Austin Stone Community Church is 10 years old. Those 10 years have gone by so quickly. It seems like yesterday I was just starting this good work.

But here's my confession. My daughter, Annie, was born right around the time we planted the church, and I have almost no memories of my sweet little girl's first two years of life. That fact devastates me. I was so involved with planting my church, so consumed with making sure everything ran smoothly, so absorbed in pursuing my goal and creating a successful ministry, that I missed out on an important part of my princess's young life. In pursuing success as a pastor, I was failing as a father.

My wife is a down-to-earth Southern beauty who doesn't pull punches, so she'll tell you that I flat-out ignored my family for several years. It's not that I didn't love my wife and kids; it's just that I was consumed with my job and it stole my rightful allegiances.

Thankfully, I've reconciled things with my family in recent years, and I've brought my life more into balance. But I think my story is a common one, which is why I need to ask the question: Men, why do things like this happen? Why, in our quest for success and achievement, do we so easily lose sight of what's most important? Some of your fathers may be guilty of the same thing. That's why it is so important to properly understand what a real win looks like. I think you'll agree that succeeding in business and failing as a husband or father isn't winning.

Just because you aren't a father or husband yet, you may be guilty of similar pursuits. Ask yourself a couple questions:

- What are some things you've done to get better grades that you would normally say are wrong?
- What are some shortcuts you have taken to get ahead?
- How many times have you gone against your own beliefs to be accepted?

I think idolatry is the often-overlooked answer to many of these questions. It's the root that drives us toward unrealistic and unfulfilling definitions of success. That was true of me, and I believe it's true of many other guys today. Maybe it's even true of you.

Let's explore that concept together and find out.

Which of the previous questions bothered you the most as you honestly answered it? Why?

What steps can you take to repair damage done or to prevent yourself from repeating the mistake again?

What ultimately were you seeking that made you go against what you knew to be right?

UNDERSTANDING IDOLATRY

Most of us understand from history and archaeology that in ancient cultures, people worshiped physical idols. They created a statue or carving out of wood, metal, or stone, and then they bowed down in front of their creation and worshiped it as a god. They even went so far as to slaughter animals or their own children and burn them as offerings to these idols.

That sounds so ridiculous. For those of us living in a modern, Western culture, the idea of worshiping something we built with our own hands seems crazy. We understand what the prophet Isaiah was getting at when he wrote these words about an idolater. Check out the following Scripture passage.

He cuts down cedars... Then it becomes fuel for a man. He takes a part of it and warms himself; he kindles a fire and bakes bread. Also he makes a god and worships it; he makes it an idol and falls down before it. Half of it he burns in the fire. Over the half he eats meat; he roasts it and is satisfied. Also he warms himself and says, "Aha, I am warm, I have seen the fire!" And the rest of it he makes into a god, his idol, and falls down to it and worships it. He prays to it and says, "Deliver me, for you are my god!"
ISAIAH 44:14-17

How would you summarize Isaiah's main point in these verses?

What motivates people to create their own paths to God, forgiveness, and salvation?

Basically, most of us think of idols and idolatry as ideas that are kind of out there—concepts that don't have any application to our everyday lives. Unfortunately, we're wrong. That's because the definition of idolatry isn't limited to worshiping a physical idol. Rather, a more comprehensive definition of idolatry is:

PURSUING ANYTHING MORE THAN YOU PURSUE GOD. It's worshiping or desiring anything more than you worship and desire God.

How do your thoughts about idolatry change after reading this definition? Why?

Idolatry is a major problem in today's society. It's a major problem even within the church and among those of us attempting to follow Jesus. Why? Because it's so easy for us to drift into pursuing our own definitions of success or our own desires more than we pursue God and what He's planned for us.

And when that happens—when idolatry takes up residence in our hearts—it becomes more destructive to our souls than we can possibly imagine. If you don't believe that, look back at what King Solomon had to say in the Book of Ecclesiastes.

Solomon was the wisest and most successful man of his day. He had everything: money, power, fame, and respect. He ate the best foods, drank the best wine, wore the best clothes, and listened to the best music. He even had a harem filled with hundreds of the most beautiful women in the land. He literally became the most powerful man in the world, and he was denied nothing he desired. Here's what he ultimately concluded about the whole situation:

> I the Preacher have been king over Israel in Jerusalem. And I applied my heart to seek and to search out by wisdom all that is done under heaven. It is an unhappy business that God has given to the children of man to be busy with. I have seen everything that is done under the sun, and behold, all is vanity and a striving after wind.
> **ECCLESIASTES 1:12-14**

What's your initial reaction to these verses? Why?

Do you agree or disagree with Solomon's conclusion? Explain.

You'd think a man who had it all would be supremely happy—that he'd feel content, satisfied, and respected, as if he had it all together. But in the end Solomon determined that all he had accumulated and experienced was worthless. He had it all and felt as if he had nothing.

How have you seen Solomon's experience play out in the life of someone you know?

Have you ever pursued something you desperately wanted, and when you got it, it wasn't what you thought it would be?

Later in Ecclesiastes, Solomon explained why none of his pursuits and achievements could bring satisfaction:

> I have seen the business that God has given to the children of man to be busy with. He has made everything beautiful in its time. Also, he has put eternity into man's heart, yet so that he cannot find out what God has done from the beginning to the end.
> **ECCLESIASTES 3:10-11**

That word *eternity* is the key to this verse. Solomon realized that God has placed in every human heart a longing for something that really matters—something that's eternal. And who or what is eternal? *God.*

Whether or not we realize it, all of us are fueled by a built-in longing for eternity—for God. And for that reason we won't be satisfied by anything that isn't eternal. We can't find fulfillment or purpose in anything that isn't God Himself.

That's why idolatry is so destructive. It pushes us to pursue non-eternal things more than we pursue God. It drives us to spend our lives striving for people, possessions, or accomplishments that can't ever fill the deepest needs of our hearts.

IDOLATRY AND YOU

COLT'S STORY

I know I've struggled with idolatry in the past, and I'm sure I'll continue feeling the urge to run away from God and pursue things that are ultimately unimportant. For me, that's typically involved the idol of power.

For example, toward the end of my college football career, there was a lot of talk saying that I was in a good position to be drafted, maybe even in the first round. That's certainly something I was striving for. But after my injury in the BCS National Championship game, there were concerns about my shoulder holding up over the long haul. So instead of achieving my goal of being a first-round pick, I ended up getting drafted in the third round.

Now being a third-round pick in the NFL is certainly a great opportunity, and I really don't mean to complain, but it wasn't all I was hoping for. There are lots of reasons my situation grated on me. Honestly, one of them was financial. The difference between my salary as a third-round pick and that of a first-round pick was literally millions of dollars. More importantly, there were 84 guys drafted ahead of me by NFL teams. That hurt my pride.

Again, I was struggling with the pursuit of power—with my desire to be the best. The draft results made it clear that I wasn't the man anymore; I wasn't on top, even on my own team. Also, I felt a little disappointed in God. I felt that this was another situation in which I was set up to receive a blessing, but I was ultimately let down.

Things didn't get any easier my first year with the Cleveland Browns. My head coach, Eric Mangini, told me that he'd never had a rookie quarterback play for him, so he wanted my first year to be a watching-and-learning year. Our starting quarterback was the talented Jake Delhomme, and his backup was Seneca Wallace, a nine-year veteran of the NFL. That meant I wasn't going to play.

For a guy who'd been the starting quarterback at the University of Texas, that was a major disappointment. I hadn't missed a start in four years, but now I'd be watching our games from the sidelines.

Thankfully, God didn't waste my feelings of discontentment. As I poured myself into training each day, I began to recognize that idolatry was ultimately the source of my disappointment. I realized that all men turn to different things in an effort to feel fulfilled, valued, satisfied, or relieved, and I was trying to pursue power.

I thought if I could just get on top and be the best, everything would get better. But through prayer, studying the Scripture, and conversations with Matt, I finally understood that only God could satisfy the strongest desires inside me. Unless I turned to Him, I'd continue to feel disappointed, no matter how successful my career became.

I love being an NFL quarterback. I couldn't be happier about getting to practice and train and go hard with my teammates every day. But if my heart had been set only on winning games, winning awards, and being the best, I'd have been on the verge of despair more than once in recent years.

Achievement is still important to me, of course. I want to win. I get up every day and work my tail off to become a successful quarterback, and I hope something great is going to happen as I continue in my career. I'm shooting to lead my team well, be the best player I can be, and take my team to the Super Bowl someday.

But ultimately, my heart is set on something greater than all of those goals. I've realized that being a great quarterback isn't my only purpose in life; it's not even my primary purpose. Instead, my purpose is serving God and trusting Him. That involves serving my wife, leading my family, loving my teammates and coaches, reaching out to my community, and being the best follower of Christ I can be.

What secondary purposes have risen up in your life and are taking the place of your primary purpose?

How would you describe the primary purpose of your life in recent years?

CONFRONTING IDOLATRY

When you give advice to people or explain the rules in a certain situation, don't you start with the most important stuff first? That makes the most sense. And that's why we need to pay attention to God's first statement in the Ten Commandments:

> "You shall have no other gods before me. You shall not make for yourself a carved image, or any likeness of anything that is in heaven above, or that is in the earth beneath, or that is in the water under the earth. You shall not bow down to them or serve them."
> **EXODUS 20:3-5**

Think about that for a moment: God commanded His people to fight against idolatry before He commanded them not to murder one another. God talked about idolatry before He talked about adultery, stealing, or lying.

If you're still feeling that idolatry isn't that big of a deal in your life, then this needs to be the moment you give in and get with the program. Idolatry is a huge deal to God. Idolatry is present in our lives, and it's more destructive than we can imagine.

In what ways have you seen idolatry promoted by today's culture?

What pursuits have you seen in your life or in the lives of those around you, that you think are driven by idolatry?

We've talked about how destructive these idols can become in our lives. So, how do we deal with these idols? How do we confront them and actively seek to stop pursuing them?

The first step is to realize that we don't have to do this on our own. In fact, we can't do this on our own. God doesn't want us to spend our lives pursuing things that can't satisfy us, and He's willing to help. In addition, He's promised to help.

> I am sure of this, that he who began a good work in you will bring it
> to completion at the day of Jesus Christ.
> **PHILIPPIANS 1:6**

Scripture promises that God has been working in your life every day since you became a Christian to help you become more like Jesus, and He will continue working until the day you see Him face-to-face. You're not in this alone, and you don't have to rely on your own strength and willpower to step away from idols.

How have you changed since you decided to follow God?

What are you doing on a daily basis to stay connected to your Heavenly Father?

There are two ways God goes about highlighting and removing idols from our hearts.

1. **Sometimes God prevents us from experiencing the things we want so badly.** In other words, He keeps us from achieving goals that are driven by idolatry. God may withhold something you desire until you get to the place where you truly pursue Him above anything else.

2. **Sometimes God actually lets you have the thing you're longing for in order to prove that it can't meet your heart's desire.** He gives you what you want and then allows you to feel the disappointment and despair that come with realizing that you're still not satisfied. That's what happened with Solomon, of course. He had everything, and it drove him to realize that only God could satisfy his deepest desires.

When have you recently achieved a goal or fulfilled a desire that left you feeling disappointed?

Does all this mean we're supposed to sit back passively and wait for God to do the work of removing our idols? No, that's not what we're saying at all.

Our job is to pursue God with everything we have—to pour our energy and resources into trusting Him and serving Him every hour of every day. That's authentic success, and that's our best weapon in the fight against idolatry.

So, we can pursue God and fight against idolatry by studying God's Word every day—by submitting to the truths He's communicated in the Bible. We can do it by spending time in prayer throughout the day, not just when we need something or want something from God but simply to talk with Him about our dreams, fears, failures, and hopes. We can fight idolatry by practicing other spiritual disciplines such as fasting, memorizing Scripture, praising God, and more.

Our desires for popularity, control, comfort, and approval aren't wrong in and of themselves. All of these desires are proper desires if placed within the context of eternity and if submitted to the lordship of Christ. The problem comes when we try to short-circuit eternity and seek a counterfeit version of the desires God has placed in our hearts.

Idolatry is real, and we all experience it to one degree or another. Idolatry is damaging and ultimately worthless. Until we recognize the bait that is covering a painful hook, we'll continue to be unsatisfied in our pursuits. So quit pursuing your idols. Run to Jesus instead, because that's where your real win will be.

Let's finish with a verse that can help us keep in mind our primary goal of pursuing God:

> Delight yourself in the LORD,
> and he will give you the desires of your heart.
> **PSALM 37:4**

WORK

WORK OR **FUN**?

There are lots of ways to have fun in the world today, and many of them require very little effort on our part. For example, you can pick up a TV remote or a video-game controller and entertain yourself almost immediately. Or you can snatch up a football, walk into the backyard with a buddy, and play a little catch without any preparation.

When it comes to outdoor activities like hunting and fishing, however, most people have to put in a good amount of work before they can have a little fun.

For fishing it's important to find the right bait to match the fish you're trying to catch. You need to maintain your equipment and prepare your rod before going out. You need to identify the right time to fish, hitch up your boat to your trailer, and usually drive awhile to find the perfect spot. It takes work to fish.

It takes even more work to hunt. Most hunters spend hours and hours maintaining their property by filling feeders, building tree stands or blinds, and clearing out brush and branches to keep a good line of site. You have to be disciplined in maintaining your equipment. You typically have to wake up before the sun in order to hunt, and you probably have to stay up late the night before to keep things scented properly and arrange everything just right. It takes work.

So, here's a question: What's the difference between the work we put in before having fun, and the work we do in our lives every day? Why does one kind of work seem natural, positive and exciting, while schoolwork and part-time jobs so often drive us crazy?

We'll address that question and a lot of others this week as we explore this idea of work and how it helps us achieve the real win in our lives.

WORK: A QUICK HISTORY

MATT'S STORY

A while back I read a fascinating book called *Open*. It's the autobiography of Andre Agassi, one of the most recognizable tennis stars ever to play the game.

I knew from my friendship with Colt that being a professional athlete doesn't automatically mean you have an easy, carefree life. But I'd always assumed that people who dedicated their lives to a specific sport did so because they enjoyed that sport so much—especially someone like Andre Agassi, who spent more than 20 years as a pro. That makes sense, right?

But look at what Agassi had to say about his job as a tennis player:

> *My name is Andre Agassi. My wife's name is Stefanie Graf. We have two children, a son and a daughter, five and three. We live in Las Vegas, Nevada, but currently reside in a suite at the Four Seasons Hotel in New York City, because I'm playing in the 2006 U.S. Open. My last U.S. Open.*
> *In fact my last tournament ever. I play tennis for a living, even though I hate tennis, hate it with a dark and secret passion, and always have.[1]*

Isn't that incredible? I picked up the book in an airport bookstore and skimmed the first page until I saw that last sentence. I was hooked! I had to read more.

Truth be told, that's how many men feel about their work. Maybe your dad feels this way, maybe one day you will too.

I'm fortunate enough to be in a position where I really enjoy what I do for a living, but I fully understand that many men literally *hate* their jobs and many guys your age hate school and whatever work they have to do as well. They hate hearing the alarm clock go off every morning. They hate sitting in class. They hate doing homework. They want to do something different. The same struggle you feel about school doesn't go away when you get older, it just changes a bit.

Here's the good news: you don't have to feel like Andre Agassi. You don't have to hate what you do day after day. Instead, you can find joy and purpose in your work now and even one day when you feel your job isn't fun or inspiring.

That's because God invites us to follow Him wholeheartedly in every area of our lives, including how we prepare for the future and the jobs you will work to make a living.

Record three things you enjoy working on right now:

1.

2.

3.

What type of work do you think you will enjoy doing in the future?

How can you keep that job from becoming just a paycheck?

GOOD WORK TURNED BAD

The Bible has a lot to say about the subject of work, so we'll explore several Scripture passages over the next several pages. The best place to get started is with our friend Adam, the first man ever to land a job:

> The LORD God formed the man of dust from the ground and
> breathed into his nostrils the breath of life, and the man
> became a living creature. And the LORD God planted a garden
> in Eden, in the east, and there he put the man whom he
> had formed. The LORD God took the man and put him in the
> garden of Eden to work it and keep it.
> **GENESIS 2:7-8,15**

What do these verses teach about work?

Notice that Adam (and later Eve) was placed in the garden of Eden with a specific purpose: *to work*. He was to cultivate the plant life, and he also had dominion over the animals, even to the point of giving a name to every living thing he encountered (see Gen. 2:19).

Also notice that Adam's call to work came in Genesis 2. Why is that important? Because sin didn't enter the world until Genesis 3, a chapter later. In other words, God commanded Adam to get to work while everything was still unblemished and perfect. Work was part of God's plan from the beginning.

Don't miss the significance of that fact. So often we think of work as something evil or as punishment for Adam's sin. We think before the fall Adam and Eve were just lying around all day, eating fruit and being naked. But the truth is that they were working, even at the beginning. And it was a good thing. Work isn't evil. Work isn't punishment for sin or a by-product of the fall. No, work is ordained by God.

What's your reaction to the previous statements?

Unfortunately, that wasn't the end of the story. The fall happened. Sin entered the world and corrupted everything, including work. Here's what God said to Adam in Genesis 3:

> "Because you have listened to the voice of your wife
> and have eaten of the tree
> of which I commanded you, 'You shall not eat of it,'
> cursed is the ground because of you;
> in pain you shall eat of it all the days of your life;
> thorns and thistles it shall bring forth for you;
> and you shall eat the plants of the field.
> By the sweat of your face
> you shall eat bread,
> till you return to the ground,
> for out of it you were taken;
> for you are dust,
> and to dust you shall return."
> **GENESIS 3:17-19**

What do these verses teach about work?

If work was originally good and part of God's plan, what purpose do you think it originally served?

List the ways sin corrupted work, according to these verses.

Do you see how drastic the change was for work before and after the fall? This is why, thousands of years later, one of the best tennis players of all time—a career athlete who made hundreds of millions of dollars playing tennis and inspiring thousands of fans the world over—would describe his work so negatively: "I play tennis for a living, even though I hate tennis, hate it with a dark and secret passion, and always have."

Fortunately, we don't have to end there.

UNDERSTANDING OUR WORK

So far we've seen that work was always part of God's plan and originally a good thing, but it was corrupted by sin along with everything else in this world. Consequently, work has become a source of drudgery, frustration, and pain for many people in the world today.

That brings us to these words from Solomon:

> I made great works. I built houses and planted vineyards for myself. I made myself gardens and parks, and planted in them all kinds of fruit trees. I made myself pools from which to water the forest of growing trees. I bought male and female slaves, and had slaves who were born in my house. I had also great possessions of herds and

flocks, more than any who had been before me in Jerusalem. **Then I considered all that my hands had done and the toil I had expended in doing it, and behold, all was vanity and a striving after wind, and there was nothing to be gained under the sun.**
ECCLESIASTES 2:4-7,11, EMPHASIS ADDED

What's your initial reaction to these verses?

Record three recent accomplishments that you're most proud of.
1.

2.

3.

How would you rate their significance? Fast forward ten years from now and ask the same question.

We emphasized Ecclesiastes 2:11 because it's something you need to wrestle with. Solomon, one of the wisest people who ever lived, achieved more through his work than most of us could even dream of accomplishing. And yet he referred to it all as vanity—like chasing the wind.

How do we keep work from being a worthless pursuit?

RECONCILING OUR WORK

If you're not familiar with that term, *reconciliation* refers to restoring something that was broken or connecting two or more things that were separated in the past. It's a term that implies fixing something that was once broken, and if there's one thing guys like to do, it is fix things.

Christians often speak of reconciliation in connection with the gospel message because that's exactly what Jesus accomplished through His death and resurrection. Our world was broken because of sin, and we as human beings were separated from God because of our rebellion against Him.

But when Jesus sacrificed Himself on the cross, He paved the way for our broken world to be restored—for the damage caused by sin to be repaired. In the same way, He gave all people a chance to become reconnected with God through His forgiveness of our sin. That's reconciliation.

Here's how Paul summarized this idea:

> In Him [Christ] all the fullness of God was pleased to dwell, and through him to reconcile to himself all things, whether on earth or in heaven, making peace by the blood of his cross.
> **COLOSSIANS 1:19-20**

In your own words, what does it mean that Jesus reconciled "all things" (v. 20) to Himself?

Maybe you're wondering, *What does all this have to do with work?* The work we do is part of the "all things" mentioned in verse 20. In other words, Jesus' sacrifice paved the way for our work to be reconciled to God just like everything else.

The gospel of Jesus Christ and the message of His cross brings purpose, value, and joy back to a man's work. Because of the gospel you're no longer forced to work in vain. Because of the cross you no longer have to chase the wind. Thanks to the reconciliation Christ provided, our work can be infused with meaning and even joy. But it doesn't just happen. We have to actively move toward and accept the redemption we've been offered in our work. Colossians 3:23-24 offers us insight into how we can keep work from becoming vain and pointless.

> Whatever you do, work heartily, as for the Lord and not for men, knowing that from the Lord you will receive the inheritance as your reward. You are serving the Lord Christ.
> **COLOSSIANS 3:23-24**

Here are three questions that will help you begin to understand the value of work, the importance of a good work ethic, and what the ultimate role of work is right now.

1. **Who do you work for?**

2. **How do you work?**

3. **What are you doing it for?**

Who do you work for? "Work heartily, as for the Lord"

You will find this out soon enough, so let's get it out of the way now: you will not always like the people you work for. Many people don't like the work they currently do and some may also feel distaste for the bosses, supervisors, and managers who oversee their work.

Thankfully, we have the option of working as if God is our boss. That phrase "as for the Lord and not for men" (v. 23) is vitally important for any guy who's seeking to find joy and purpose in his work. That's because it reminds us that God is in charge of this universe.

As the Creator and Sustainer of all things, God is aware of everything that's going on in your life, including your struggles. He sees what you're dealing with. He sees the obstacles in front of you and the frustration you experience dealing with the same problems day after day. But through it all He's reminding you to trust Him and serve Him, even at work.

HOW DO YOU WORK?

Given that God is our ultimate Boss, we can't lose sight of that first phrase from Colossians 3:23: "Whatever you do, work heartily." Think for a minute about your grades. Are you one of those guys that do just enough work to get by in class? Do you find out how to get the best grade possible by doing the least amount of work? Do you only work hard when your parents or supervisor is around?

It doesn't matter whether you go on to be the CEO of a Fortune 500 company or the low man in an organization making paper clips; God invites you to work heartily for Him. That means, when it comes to everything you do, you're called to give everything you've got.

WHAT ARE YOU DOING IT FOR?

God gives us opportunities to serve Him and demonstrate trust in Him, not simply to make money or get good grades, or make a big deal about ourselves. It is about Him.

Let's be honest: we've all been tempted to give less than 100 percent at some point. We're tempted to tap the brakes when nobody else is looking or maybe to figure out the minimum we need to do in order to get by and meet the expectations placed on us, especially when we don't feel that our extra efforts are appreciated or even noticed.

When are you tempted to give less than 100 percent...

- **At School?**

- **At Home?**

- **On the field?**

How does your lack of effort impact those around you?

How does it demonstrate your relationship with God?

Remember that in all you do, "You are serving the Lord Christ" (v. 24).

COLT'S STORY

People usually see professional football players only on game days, typically on Sundays. But have you ever wondered what guys like me do the rest of the time? Here's a quick look at my typical workweek.

During the regular season we practice on Monday. That typically involves watching film of our most recent game, both as a team and in our individual-position groups. We want to see what we did well and how we can improve.

Tuesday is our day off—our "weekend," for lack of a better word. Even so, a few players show up for a couple of hours on Tuesdays. I'm one of them. As a quarterback, I often go in on Tuesdays for a good portion of the day to get a head start on the week because I need to know what our game plan is going to be.

Every player on the team is expected to show up the rest of the week. We practice Wednesday through Friday, and those days include more film study, classroom time, and work on the field. Saturday is travel day when we have away games, but we still do a walk-through for our game plan before getting on the plane. Sunday is game day, of course, and then it starts all over again.

The average practice looks different, depending on whether you play offense or defense. Because I'm a quarterback, my day is full every day. I get to the facility about 6:00 a.m., have breakfast, look over what we're going to do for the day, then watch film, either of our previous day's practice or of our upcoming opponent. We have our regular team meeting at 9:00 a.m. Then we divide up and go into specific meetings for either offense or defense. I meet with the offensive line, the receivers, and the running backs. Then we go through a walk-through of the next set of drills and plays at 11:00 a.m.

At noon we have lunch. Right after lunch everybody gets taped up, and we all go to the field for practice. Usually we practice for 1½ to 2 hours, then come back inside for more meetings. As we watch the day's practice on film, we talk about corrections we need to make in preparation for Sunday. Right after the debriefing is finished, I go to the weight room, or if I'm injured, I go to the training room for treatment.

Is this what you would have imagined my week looked like?

On most days I go home around 6:00 p.m. For me, work means a long day every day. I'm not just a guy who walks out onto the field on Sunday, plays a game, then does nothing the rest of the week. I have to work just like you, and it's tough. It can even be a grind.

Thankfully, I had good teachers at home and at church who encouraged me early on to "work heartily, as for the Lord and not for men." In fact, Colossians 3:23 has been my favorite verse for years. I still have bad days, of course. I still get frustrated and disappointed when things don't go my way or when I run up against tough situations.

But eventually, I always come back to the fact that God is my ultimate Boss, and I work for Him in everything I do.

Think about your school week like a workweek. Describe some of the best parts of your current workweek.

What parts of your workweek are more frustrating or difficult to handle?

Do you see yourself working for God in everything you do? Why or why not? What needs to change in order for you to adopt that attitude?

1. Andre Agassi, *Open: An Autobiography* (New York: Knopf, 2009), 3.

PURSUIT

MOVING **CLOSER**

If you've ever hunted a deer, you know there are basically two options when it comes to your choice of weapons: a gun or a bow. The overall experience of the hunt is similar with both weapons; you still have to prepare in advance, know your location, and make a good shot when an opportunity presents itself.

But there's one major difference between hunting with a gun and hunting with a bow: distance. With a decent long-range rifle it's reasonable to shoot a deer at a range of 200 yards or more, sometimes even 300 yards. That means you can set up a tree stand at the edge of a cornfield or another wide-open space where there's deer traffic and just wait. If you see a target as many as two or three football fields away, you can still make the shot and harvest the animal.

Bow hunting is much more intimate. The maximum range for a kill shot with most modern bows is 50 yards, and that's pushing it. To have a reasonable chance at a successful hunt, you probably need to keep your shot to under 30 yards—not even 100 feet.

In other words, bow hunting requires a much closer pursuit of the deer. It forces you to be more intentional and more deliberate in your approach. You have to know the animal's needs and habits in order to get close enough for a successful shot.

As we'll see this week, distance is also an important principle when it comes to a man's relationship with his wife. As you prepare for that time in your life, you will need to learn that you must pursue your future wife even after you are married. The pursuit doesn't end when you get married. In many ways, it only just begins with marriage.

PREPARING FOR MARRIAGE

MATT'S STORY

As you think about what marriage might be like, let me tell you a story that will help you understand the challenges you will face.

Here's something you might not hear every day: one of the most important turning points in my marriage was sparked by my wife's encounter with another man. I'll get to that story in a minute, but first some background.

I've been married for 16 years as of the writing of this study, and I was a miserable failure as a husband for the first 10, so much so that my wife became despondent because of our relationship. And you know what's really pathetic? I had no idea anything was wrong.

During the first decade of our life together, Jennifer and I almost never argued. My wife is a laid-back person who doesn't complain. She loves and follows Jesus. So in many ways she was doing fine without my leading her or engaging with her as I should have. Meanwhile, I went happily along thinking everything was all right.

To be honest, I felt our marriage was smooth because I was a rock-star husband. I thought I had everything figured out.

Then one day my wife sat down with me to talk, but before she could get any words out, she broke down in tears. When she was finally able to speak, she said, "Matt, I want you to understand that I'd never leave you or cheat on you. But our marriage just isn't working right now."

I was shocked. "What do you mean, Jenn? What's going on?" Remember, I thought I was one of the best husbands around.

"Even when you're here, Matt, you're just not *here*," she said. "We're distant, and I never feel connected to you. When we were dating, you totally pursued me. But when we got married, you stopped pursuing me." Then she got to the heart of her feelings: "You pursue the church. You pursue your work. But you don't pursue *me*."

I was still trying to get my mind around what she was saying, so I asked for an example. Jenn was quiet for a long time. Then she told me something that had happened on a recent Sunday morning after church.

It had already been a full morning, and she was walking out to our car with our three young children in tow, plus a stroller, a diaper bag, and all the other stuff young moms need to cart around when they have little kids. I was off somewhere else, as usual, busy with church stuff, but a well-meaning man saw she was struggling to juggle everything and offered to help. He opened her car door and helped corral our kids into the backseat.

This guy did everything a good husband should have done in that situation. Nothing more happened. The guy said, "Have a good day" and walked away.

"I'd never ever cheat on you," Jenn repeated as she told me the story, "but I want you to know how good it felt for a man to pay attention to me."

At that moment I realized for the first time how poor a husband I'd been. I'd emotionally neglected my wife to the point that a simple act of kindness from a random man filled an empty place in her heart. Our conversation woke me up in a big way, and I realized there's a lot more to being a good husband than I'd considered.

What do you think it will take to be a good husband?

What have you been taught by your family or church about being a good husband?

WHAT WOMEN NEED

You can hardly turn on the TV without encountering an exaggerated example of husbands in today's culture. These men are usually exaggerated in one of two directions: they're either total buffoons or perfect gentlemen.

The total-buffoon husbands are the guys who do the right thing only by accident. These guys are typically overweight, have foul mouths, and don't care about anyone or anything, except how to get their hands on the next can of beer. Homer Simpson is a good example of a total-buffoon husband.

On the other end of the spectrum, some husbands portrayed in movies and TV shows are perfect gentlemen. These guys look good, dress well, and know how to pour on the charm. They say the right things and know how to make the women around them feel special. Coach Taylor from "Friday Night Lights" is a good example of a perfect-gentleman husband.

What can we learn from the way husbands are represented in today's culture? Obviously, we want to avoid acting like the buffoonish guys who think only about themselves and provoke contempt in the minds of their future wives and families.

But we can also glean information from the behavior of those perfect-gentlemen husbands. Specifically, it's interesting that the men portrayed most positively in our culture are the ones who are intentional about pursuing the women they care about. These men go to great lengths to prove their love—and not just in the big things. They also do little things every day to make their women feel cherished, adored, and appreciated.

There's a deep need in the soul of every woman—whether it's a girlfriend, fiancée, wife, or daughter—to be cherished, pursued, and loved by the man God has placed in her life. Notice this is a *need,* not a want. If you'd like to be married, keep in mind that your future wife was created with a need to be pursued and cherished. She can't be herself if that need is unmet, and it's your responsibility to meet it. You can begin practicing this principle now.

How have you seen the women in your life (mother, sister, or friend) display the need to be cherished and pursued?

Who are some guys among your friends and family who do a good job of meeting that need for the women they love?

Thankfully, we don't have to depend on our culture's view of husbands to figure out what women need and how men should behave. The Bible has a lot to say about husbands and wives and a key passage for us is Ephesians 5:25. Here we will see what it looks like when a husband loves his wife.

The following words from Ray Ortlund can help us wrap our brains around the issues involved:

> In the heart of every fallen woman is the self-doubt that wonders, "Do I please you? Am I what you wanted?" A wise husband will understand that question at the center of his wife's heart. And he will spend his life answering it, communicating to her in various ways, "Darling, you are the one I need. I cherish you."[1]

That's what we mean when we talk about loving your future wife.

What can you do to prepare to love your future wife? How can you practice these things now?

The Bible gives you clear advice on how to actively, intentionally answer that question for your future wife. You'll find it here:

> The husband is the head of the wife even as Christ is the head of the church, his body, and is himself its Savior. Now as the church submits to Christ, so also wives should submit in everything to their husbands. Husbands, love your wives, as Christ loved the church and gave himself up for her, that he might sanctify her, having cleansed her by the washing of water with the word, so that he might present the church to himself in splendor, without spot or wrinkle or any such thing, that she might be holy and without blemish. In the same way husbands should love their wives as their own bodies. He who loves his wife loves himself.
> **EPHESIANS 5:23-28**

What's your initial reaction to these verses?

What do you think it means to love your wife as Christ loved the church?

A lot is contained in that Scripture passage, but let's focus on verse 25: "Husbands, love your wives, as Christ loved the church and gave himself up for her."

HUSBANDS, LOVE

Notice how the first two words of Ephesians 5:25 form a short, simple, and powerful command: "Husbands, love." That's really what the pursuit is all about. If you want to be a husband, you're called to love the woman who will give you that title.

Also notice that it's an active command. You have to *do* something in order to love. You can't demonstrate your love by doing nothing.

What kind of actions would help your future wife know that you love her?

How can you be praying for your future wife right now?

When we keep reading Ephesians 5:25, we see "Husbands, love your wives, *as Christ loved the church*" (emphasis added). That's another important point. You need to love your future wife in the same way Jesus loved the church.

One of the most important things we need to realize is that Jesus loved the church *first*. He initiated the love relationship between Himself and the church. In other words, Jesus didn't sit back with His arms folded and expect us as Christians to approach Him, love Him, serve Him, and then hope He'd love us back.

No, in spite of our dysfunctions, shortcomings, failures, and sins, Jesus initiated a relationship with us. He loved us first. He loved us in spite of everything. That's why 1 John 4:19 says, "We love because he first loved us."

Let's be honest and admit we don't naturally think this way in our relationships with other people. We expect to be loved first, and then we're willing to reciprocate with our own demonstrations of love. When you are a husband, maybe you will expect to receive respect and admiration from your wife. You may even expect to have your needs taken care of and your desires satisfied, and then you'll show your love in return. But that's not how Christ loved the church, and that's not how you're called to pursue and cherish your future wife: "Husbands, love your wives, as Christ loved the church."

On a scale of 1 to 10, how difficult do you think it will be to demonstrate love to your future wife?

1	2	3	4	5	6	7	8	9	10
Not likely									Very likely

GIVE YOURSELF

Let's finish up the instruction from Ephesians 5:25: "Husbands, love your wives, as Christ loved the church *and gave himself up for her*" (emphasis added).

As the Head of the church, Jesus could have exercised His authority in any way He wanted. But how did He lead the church? By giving Himself up for it. And in Jesus' case, specifically, He laid His life down to show love for His people and initiate a relationship with us.

When have you been in a situation that called you to put someone else's needs above your own? What happened?

You've probably never been put in a place where you needed to die for someone else. But there are a lot of other ways you can give yourself up for your future wife.

Think about personal purity, for example. As a guy, you're called to be faithful to your future wife in both mind and deed. You are called by God to wait for your future wife and for sex. You want the woman you marry to feel secure and confident in your commitment to her alone.

Therefore, you have several opportunities to sacrifice your personal freedom and flexibility for the sake of your future wife. You can make sure your phone, tablet, and personal computer are protected by software that blocks inappropriate content. You can commit to hold off on serious dating until you are ready to pursue marriage. You can commit to regularly meeting with other guys to hold one another accountable to staying pure before marriage. This group can share what you have done in preparation for your future wife when the time comes.

How would you be affected if you adopted these precautions for personal purity?

How would adopting these measures for personal purity affect your relationship with your friends and family now?

Remember that authentic success comes in this life when you trust God and serve Him. That's the real win. One of the greatest opportunities you've been given to experience that win is to trust God enough to accept His guidance for pursuing and cherishing your future wife and then to serve Him by serving her.

PREPARING TO LEAD YOUR WIFE

COLT'S STORY

I've been married since 2010, and I love my wife more than I ever thought possible. We're at a really good place in our marriage now, but it hasn't always been that way. Honestly, there have been some times when I just plain blew it as a husband.

The rockiest of those times sprang from my heavy work schedule and other job challenges. Frankly, it's been hard for me to love my wife as Christ loved the church and to serve her first when my entire world revolves around football. I've known since my first day as a husband that I'm supposed to make a priority of loving and serving my wife, but I haven't always known how best to go about it.

For example, Rachel and I went through a rough patch in relation to my behavior whenever I came home from work. During our first year together I'd arrive home from the practice facility and plop down on the couch, ready for some alone time. I was ready for dinner when I got home, but I kept telling myself I didn't have the energy to engage with my wife or interact with her after a hard day.

Things finally got to the point where Rachel asked to sit down with me and have a talk. Her personality is super sweet, but she still made it clear that I wasn't living up to the expectations she had for me as a husband. "With the amount of time you spend on football," she said, "it's like I don't even have a husband."

That hurt.

I've since learned that quality time is one of my wife's main love languages. So today I make a greater effort to spend time with her and talk with her intentionally. I ask, "How are you doing? How was your day? What went on today? Whom have you talked to? How's your family? How's my family? How's your walk with Jesus?" Our conversations together have become much more meaningful. I know she appreciates the change, and so do I.

A more difficult example of my struggles as a husband has been the area of prayer. Now I pray a lot. I pray before I go to bed, at meals, and during my quiet times with the Lord. I even pray sometimes in the middle of games. But for some reason, I struggled to pray with my wife early in our marriage.

As a new husband, I knew I was supposed to pray with my wife. I'd read and heard in sermons for years that praying as a married couple is essential, but when we sat down together to eat or lay down together at night, for some reason I just couldn't bring myself to say the words. Basically, I was aware of what I needed to do, but I lacked the courage and the know-how to make it happen.

These days my marriage is at a better place both relationally and spiritually. But I don't think my struggles as a husband are unique. In fact, I think most guys could use a little instruction on how to be the husbands God wants us to be. It's not that marriage is a huge burden or that our wives are unlovable. It's just that we need guidance on how best to love and cherish our wives in a way that meets their needs and answers the secret questions in their hearts.

So let's finish this week by exploring what it means to love your future wife as you plan to fulfill your role as the spiritual leader in your home.

> **When have you been able to overcome a difficult time or relationship? How can you apply this to your future relationship with your wife?**

> **What are some areas in which you still have room for improvement that you could work on now before you get married?**

> **What ideas or images come to mind when you hear the phrase** *spiritual leader?*

SPIRITUAL LEADERSHIP

We're finishing our fifth week looking at the real win—the idea that we experience authentic success in life by trusting God and committing to serve Him. This week we've seen how preparing to be a great husband will involve actively loving your wife and pursuing her heart day after day. But how do those ideas connect to the real win? What does preparing to love and cherish your wife have to do with authentic success?

There are two ways to answer that question, and the first is pretty basic: God has commanded you through His Word to love your future wife "as Christ loved the church and gave himself up for her" (Eph. 5:25); therefore, you obey God's command when you love and cherish the woman He places in your care.

The second way to answer that question is to recognize that the best gift you can give your future wife is to help her experience authentic success for herself.

If you get married, understand that God has called you as a husband to be the spiritual leader in your home. It's your responsibility to support, encourage, and lead your wife and children as they seek to trust God and serve Him with you. That's what it means to be a spiritual leader in the home.

Who are some men you know who do a great job of serving as the spiritual leaders in their homes?

We've already discussed the idea of loving your future wife as Christ loved the church, but these verses get more complicated. What do they mean, and what do they have to do with your future wife?

Understand that "the washing of water" (v. 26) isn't talking about baptism. Rather, it refers to an ancient bridal practice. When this passage was written, the women in a bridal party would wash a bride-to-be with water before she was married. This ritual was primarily symbolic. It meant the bride was ready to be presented to her groom. She was clean, pure, and spotless in his sight.

As a husband, you will be called to do the same thing as the spiritual leader in your home. You will have a responsibility to ensure and support the purity of your future wife—morally, spiritually, mentally, and emotionally. This doesn't happen with actual water, of course, but with "the word" (v. 26). In other words, you don't seek to purify her with your own ideas and opinions. Rather, you ensure and nurture her purity by exposing her to the truths revealed by God in the Bible.

What's your response to the previous statements? Why?

What can you be doing right now that will help you prepare to be the spiritual leader of your wife and family?

In the space below, or on another sheet of paper, write a prayer asking God to shape you and prepare you to be a godly husband.

Many of the practices you put in place right now will enable you to lead well later in life. Don't think you are going to magically wake up one day and know the Bible well if you aren't spending time studying it now. Don't think you will become a man of prayer if you don't pray now. This whole discussion about marriage, children, and family may not seem relevant for you today, but what you do today affects how you will lead in the future.

You recognize this in other areas of your life. You practice in the offseason so you will be prepared when the season arrives. You spend hours in the gym preparing for that one moment during the game. Don't waste your days. Recognize them as a gift and an opportunity to prepare yourself for the future.

1. Ray Ortlund, "Husband and Wife," *The Gospel Coalition* [online], 13 February 2010 [cited 5 April 2013]. Available from the Internet: *http://thegospelcoalition.org.*
2. Paraphrased from Gary Chapman, *The Five Love Languages* (Chicago: Northfield Publishing, 1992).

LEGACY

MAKING **MEMORIES**

Would you agree there's something magical about the first time we accomplish something significant or achieve a desired goal? Think about your first kiss, for example, or the first time you saw the ocean or made a snowball. What kinds of memories do you still carry from your first home run or touchdown? What about your first car?

A hunter may harvest dozens of animals over the course of his life, and there's no way he can remember the detailed story surrounding each kill. But he *will* remember the first time he saw an animal go down because he pulled the trigger or released his bow.

A fisherman can literally pull hundreds of fish from the water over decades spent on docks, in boats, and on the banks of rivers and lakes. He probably couldn't remember all of the different species he's caught when his fishing career is over, but he *will* remember that thrilling moment when for the first time he pulled back on his rod, set the hook, and reeled in a fish.

One reason these first times create such powerful memories is that they can't be repeated. You can never have another first catch, first kill, or first kiss.

We'll focus on this concept of memory during our final week of study, specifically in terms of the desire each of us has to be remembered for what we've accomplished. We'll also explore God's calling for each of us to make an impact for eternity as we try to understand what it means to leave a legacy of authentic success.

THE BEST LEGACY

COLT'S STORY

In October 2010, the University of Texas awarded me a great and unexpected honor: it officially retired my number 12 jersey. That means no other Texas Longhorn will ever wear my number for as long as the Texas football program exists. I didn't fully understand what a big deal this was until I learned that only five other football players in the history of the University of Texas have had their jerseys retired. I'd joined a select group.

Quite frankly, the award surprised me when I first heard about it. I felt grateful and proud about what I'd been able to accomplish for my team and my school. The award also got me thinking about my legacy, both in sports and in life.

In the world of sports, the term *legacy* has pretty specific connotations. Your legacy as an athlete is all about your statistics and accomplishments on the field. These are the things fans talk about when they're trying to figure out whether someone belongs in the Pro Bowl or the Hall of Fame.

But when I think about my legacy as a person and especially as a follower of Jesus, things like having my jersey retired and whatever else I'm able to accomplish in the NFL won't be at the top of my list. Instead, I hope I'll be remembered for efforts and achievements that have eternal value.

Here's an example ... when I was at the University of Texas, several guys from our football team started meeting together to study the Bible and encourage one another as followers of Christ. We didn't have a chaplain or an official leader; we just knew it was best for us to support one another in community.

In one meeting we were studying Matthew 5, and we came across this verse:

> "You are the light of the world.
> A city set on a hill cannot be hidden."
> **MATTHEW 5:14**

One guy in our group said, "I've heard that term before—*COAH*. It stands for *city on a hill*. That's what I want to be like."

We asked him what he meant, and he explained that he wanted to live differently. He didn't want his identity to be based on the fact that he was a Texas football player. He wanted to be known as a person who follows Jesus.

The rest of us thought that sounded right on, so we started calling one another COAHs to remind ourselves that we had the ability to be examples and role models. Football is huge in Texas, but that wasn't the core of our identity. This title reminded us to remove any swagger that might be present in our lives. We wanted to set the standard and be the light God wanted us to be.

Pretty soon other guys started joining the study, and several of them didn't have much experience with church or the Bible. One night after practice we were meeting, and the subject of baptism came up. Lots of guys had different opinions, and a few of the new guys had no idea what we were talking about. So we dove into the Scriptures and started figuring out what it means to be baptized and why all Christians should be baptized as a public declaration of their faith. I'd been baptized when I was 14, so I was able to share my experiences with the group.

In the middle of that discussion, five guys in the group decided they wanted to be baptized—and they wanted it to happen right away! There just happened to be a pool around the corner from our practice facility, so we headed over there.

I ended up baptizing all five of those guys that night. It was an incredible experience. Obviously, it didn't happen because of anything I did or didn't do; it was the Holy Spirit working in that community of guys. They wanted to fully submit their lives to Christ and obey what the Bible commanded. I'll never forget it.

In the grand scheme of things, people might remember my football career for a few decades after I retire. Having my jersey retired by the University of Texas might keep my name in people's minds after I die, but who knows how long I'll actually be remembered? People might not even play football a hundred years from now!

But what happened at the pool that night was different because it was eternally significant. My name won't be remembered, but the consequences of baptizing five of my friends and teammates will still be felt thousands and thousands of years from now. That's the kind of legacy I want to leave.

What are some of your most impressive accomplishments so far in life? List two.

1.

2.

How have you been eternally influenced by the efforts of other people?

What are you currently investing in that has the potential to be eternally significant?

REMEMBERED OR FORGOTTEN?

Have you ever heard of Count Ludwig von Zinzendorf? The name sounds like a vampire hunter from Transylvania, but he was actually a German church leader who lived in the mid-1700s. Zinzendorf was extremely talented and dedicated to ministry. He wrote and taught extensively; worked with orphans; established communities of faith worldwide; and wrote a large number of hymns, many of which are still sung today.

If anyone deserves to be remembered for the things they did in service to Christ, Count Ludwig von Zinzendorf should be in the conversation. But that wasn't what Zinzendorf wanted:

The missionary must seek nothing for himself: no seat of honour, no report of fame. Like the cab-horses in London, the Count said, he must wear blinders and be blind to every danger and to every snare and conceit. He must be content to suffer, to die and be forgotten.[1]

Count Zinzendorf didn't work so that people would remember his good deeds. He worked, ministered, and loved the people around him so that they'd remember Jesus. That's the kind of legacy we're talking about this week.

What ideas or images come to mind when you hear the word *legacy*?

How does our culture define a successful legacy for modern men?

Most guys have a built-in desire to strive and succeed. We want to climb mountains and achieve goals. We want to perform well at whatever we do, but sometimes that desire leads us to an unhealthy craving for success and recognition. In other words, it's natural for us to think of our legacy in terms of our achievements and accomplishments.

But that's not the legacy we should be shooting for as followers of Christ. Instead, we need to be faithful in pursuing authentic success—faithful in trusting God and serving Him wherever we are and in whatever we do. Who cares whether we're remembered or forgotten as long as we finish the work God gives us?

On a scale of 1 to 10, how often do you think about the way others will remember you when you're gone from this world?

1	2	3	4	5	6	7	8	9	10
Almost never									Almost daily

Jesus Himself set the pattern for this kind of selflessness when pursuing the real win. Look at these words by the apostle Paul:

> Have this mind among yourselves, which is yours in Christ Jesus,
> who, though he was in the form of God, did not count equality with
> God a thing to be grasped, but made himself nothing, taking the form

of a servant, being born in the likeness of men. And being found in human form, he humbled himself by becoming obedient to the point of death, even death on a cross. Therefore God has highly exalted him and bestowed on him the name that is above every name, so that at the name of Jesus every knee should bow, in heaven and on earth and under the earth, and every tongue confess that Jesus Christ is Lord, to the glory of God the Father.

PHILIPPIANS 2:5-11

What strikes you as most interesting about this passage? Why?

How did Jesus demonstrate humility and selflessness in His life?

When Jesus died on the cross, it didn't look like He'd left much of a legacy. He'd written no books and accumulated no wealth. The authorities had trashed His reputation. The crowds had disappeared, and His remaining followers scattered and were ready to return to what they'd been doing before they met Jesus. But Jesus was faithful in the redemptive work He'd been called to do. And through that faithfulness He changed the world—forever.

Don't miss verse 5 in that passage, which says we're supposed to have the same mind as Jesus—the same determination to be selflessly faithful to God and His plans. That's what a true legacy looks like.

It's not about our being remembered or our names being passed through history. Instead, the best legacy we can leave behind is to be faithful to our calling, serve God selflessly, and trust that He will take care of everything else.

DEFINE YOUR LEGACY

If you've spent time studying the Bible, you've noticed that it often conflicts with the values and principles typically held by the culture around us.

For example, today's culture tells us that life is all about living life to the fullest, having the most fun possible, and making the most of each day. But the Bible calls us to deny ourselves (see Matt. 16:24). Today's culture tells us that money and possessions are the keys to happiness, and the more we have, the better our lives will be. The Bible, however, teaches that the love of money is the root of all kinds of evil (see 1 Tim. 6:10) and that we shouldn't love the things of this world (see 1 John 2:15).

What are some other areas in which the Bible conflicts with the values of society?

The same thing happens when we think about legacy. Society tells us that people are remembered and valued for their accomplishments and the impressive goals they achieve—that the ultimate goal is to achieve greatness and be remembered for generations.

But as we saw earlier, a biblical view of legacy means being faithful to God's calling. It means embracing being forgotten so that Christ can be remembered.

John Piper does a good job of summing up the Bible's perspective on legacy:
God created us to live with a single passion: to joyfully display his supreme excellence in all the spheres of life. The wasted life is the life without this passion. God calls us to pray and think and dream and plan and work not to be made much of, but to make much of him in every part of our lives.[2]

Whom do you know who demonstrates a genuine passion for God?

How would you describe our culture's view of a wasted life?

If we agree that achieving a legacy of authentic success means remaining faithful to our calling, we have to ask, how do we know our calling? How do we figure out the work we're supposed to do in order to glorify Christ?

We'll focus on your specific calling as an individual later. First, let's explore two broad callings that apply to every guy, including you.

BE A CITY ON A HILL

One way we leave a legacy that glorifies Christ is by living as a city on a hill in this world. Again, that idea comes from Jesus' teaching in Matthew 5:

> "You are the light of the world. A city set on a hill cannot be hidden.
> Nor do people light a lamp and put it under a basket, but on a stand,
> and it gives light to all in the house. In the same way, let your light
> shine before others, so that they may see your good works and give
> glory to your Father who is in heaven."
> **MATTHEW 5:14-16**

What does it mean for Christians to be "the light of the world" (v. 14)?

How do we, as Christians, "let [our] light shine before others" (v. 16)?

Just because your ultimate legacy isn't to gain personal fame doesn't mean you'll never be *noticed* in this world. Quite the opposite. Christians aren't called to live hidden, solitary lives where people don't see us and don't know we follow Christ.

Instead, we're called to live in the real world with all sorts of people from all sorts of backgrounds and faith persuasions. Our call is to live in such a way that the light of Christ shines out from us. That means going into our churches and communities and doing the kind of work that makes a difference: loving the unlovable, ministering to widows and orphans, standing against evil, feeding the hungry, visiting prisoners, sharing the good news of Jesus, and so on.

What are some problems in your community that could be helped or solved by you and your friends for the sake of Christ? List three.
1.

2.

3.

How can you pitch in to work on one or more of those problems?

According to God's Word, the work we do should be so radical that we stand out from all other people the way a brightly lit city stands out against the night sky. We should be noticed as Christians. But because our efforts focus on serving God instead of ourselves, we'll be noticed in such a way that people "see [our] good works and give glory to [our] Father who is in heaven" (v. 16).

To be a city on a hill means we reflect God's excellence and glory in every area of our lives. That's how we become "content to suffer, to die and be forgotten," as Count Zinzendorf talked about. That's how we live for the sake of Christ even as we do the hard work for His kingdom.

DEFINE YOUR CALLING

MATT'S STORY

For a long time I had no idea I'd become a pastor. In fact, I didn't want to be a pastor; I mostly planned on being a doctor when I grew up. That's the career path I would've chosen for myself.

As I began to mature, however, I eventually sensed that God wanted me to go into full-time vocational ministry. I don't remember exactly when I became aware of God's leading me in that direction; it was a gradual thing. I came to understand that He wanted me to be a pastor and wanted me to preach.

Even so, I didn't change my plans right away. I fought against what I knew He wanted. And honestly, the reason I resisted God's call was that I didn't want to be poor.

During the summer between my sophomore and junior years of college, things finally came to a head. I was working for a construction company in Texarkana at the time, and I drove back to Dallas every chance I got to see this girl named Jennifer, my future wife. So I had a lot of time to think that summer.

One afternoon I was driving on the freeway when I found myself praying and wrestling with God in a serious way. I knew He wanted me to surrender. I knew He wanted me to change the direction of my life, and I knew I didn't want to do it. I fought against giving up control and going where God was calling me to go.

Then this song came on the radio. It was a Christian song, and I'll admit parts of it were pretty cheesy. But in that moment God powerfully spoke to my heart through the words of that song.

One line in particular pointedly asked whether the listener would be the one to answer the call. And I knew God was asking that question of me. Directly. He wasn't going to let me waffle back and forth any longer. I had to make a choice.

That's when I finally surrendered. I pulled off the road and prayed to God right then and there and prayed, "Lord, I don't care where You want me to go or what You want me to do. I'm Yours. I'll do whatever You want."

That was the moment when I stopped fighting. God had been working on me and preparing me, and eventually He brought me to the place where I laid down my will and picked up His will, whatever may come.

What are some of your life goals? List three.
1.

2.

3.

When have you wrestled with God or resisted His will in the past? What happened?

To what degree have you communicated with God about your future career?

LISTEN FOR HIS CALL

As we've seen, every guy has a calling to be faithful in two broad categories: serving as a city on a hill and serving as the spiritual leader. No matter what else happens in our lives, we're doing the right thing if we focus on those two goals.

But guys also have a calling from God—something God has uniquely designed them to do or accomplish. For example, Colt McCoy's calling is to serve as a professional quarterback, at least for the next several years. Matt Carter's calling is to serve as the pastor of a church. What about you?

How would you describe your calling in life?

Does the current trajectory of your life and education match that specific calling? Explain.

Many guys feel they aren't sure about their calling. They don't know exactly what God has gifted them to do in this life. And that's OK—for a time. It often takes time for us to learn enough about ourselves and experience enough to identify the specific work God wants us to do.

But eventually we need to make some tough decisions and take up the call to do what God wants us to do. Eventually you need to fulfill your calling.

The Bible says in several places that God gives spiritual gifts to His followers in order to equip them for work in His kingdom. Romans 12:4-8 is a good example:

> As in one body we have many members, and the members do not all have the same function, so we, though many, are one body in Christ, and individually members one of another. Having gifts that differ according to the grace given to us, let us use them: if prophecy, in proportion to our faith; if service, in our serving; the one who teaches, in his teaching; the one who exhorts, in his exhortation; the one who contributes, in generosity; the one who leads, with zeal; the one who does acts of mercy, with cheerfulness.

Circle all of the specific gifts listed in the previous verses. Which of your friends and family members demonstrate these gifts?

What specific gifts has God given you to serve Him and minister to others?

It's OK if you're not sure what your specific gifts are at this time. Just continue to faithfully seek God and serve Him. As you do so, you'll begin to see how God has uniquely gifted you for His service.

Keep in mind that none of us create or force our calling in life. This is something God places on our minds and hearts. He initiates the call, and we respond.

Yet it's still possible for you to position yourself to know what God is saying to you and respond when that moment of calling comes. So even if you're not sure what God wants you to do in this moment, make sure you're working for Him. Obey His Word and focus on things that have eternal significance, and you'll be in a good place to hear Him when He's ready to give you a specific type of work.

If you're not sure about your calling in life, use the following steps to prepare yourself for God's call so that you can respond appropriately.

- **Inquire.** Begin by asking yourself, *Am I living for me, or am I living for the Lord?* If you're living for the Lord, that's awesome. If you're living for yourself, pray for transformation and take the steps God reveals to you in His Word and through prayer.

- **Surrender.** Stop wrestling with God. Get to a place where you say, "This is not about me, Lord. It's about You, and I'll do whatever You want me to do." You might not know exactly what you need to do, but you can put yourself in a position of surrender so that you're willing to do whatever God requires of you.

- **Prepare.** If you sense the Lord may be calling you in a specific direction, you might take classes in that area, read books, learn a new skill, or hone an existing skill to prepare to launch into your calling.

- **Wait.** Wait actively and expectantly, with great faith. Psalm 46:10 encourages us to "Cease striving and know that I am God" (NASB). Only God knows what will happen to you after that. He's writing your story even now, so you don't have to figure out your vision. God will reveal it to you. Seek His will through diligent Bible study and prayer.

- **Launch.** Put your seatbelt on. When God places a call on your heart, go. Be obedient. Be courageous. Choose to follow God fully, without reservations.

Circle the stage that best describes your current stage in identifying your call. What are you doing in that stage to listen for God's voice and to seek His will?

Remember, the real win is built on two simple but strategic commitments: whom we trust and whom we serve. Those two decisions change everything for a guy. When we wholeheartedly trust and serve God, we can be confident that He will lead us into a calling that will bring glory to Him and make an impact for eternity.

When it comes to legacy, it ultimately doesn't matter whether we're successful in the eyes of the world. It doesn't matter whether we fulfill the kinds of goals that fit on spreadsheets or lead to earthly fame. In Christ our hearts are satisfied.

THE REAL WINNER

Throughout this study we've talked about the real win—how to live our lives according to God's plan by trusting and serving Him. It should be clear by now that not only is there a real win in the way we live our lives, but there's also a Real Winner in the larger scope of things. Of course, the Real Winner is God.

In the grand scheme of history—from the garden, where Adam first set us guys on our course of struggle with masculinity, to the distant future long after we've fulfilled our legacy—God is working to bring His perfect plan to completion. And we know from Scripture that Christ will ultimately conquer in all things. Heaven will come to earth, and everything will be made right. Forever.

God is the great Winner, so it's appropriate that we use our lives to magnify His glory. It only makes sense for us to cast away our limited plans and definitions of success in order to submit to His perfect plan. When we trust and serve Him, we become part of the greatest victory of all.

So go for the real win. Be faithful, be a leader, win the victory over idolatry, win at school, win at home, and win the future by leaving a legacy for God's glory. If a quarterback and a preacher from Texas can find authentic success in God, you can too. We're excited to think about all God is going to do in your life, and through you, in the lives of many more people around you.

1. A. J. Lewis, *Zinzendorf, the Ecumenical Pioneer* (London: SCM Press Ltd., 1962), 92.
2. John Piper, *Don't Waste Your Life* (Wheaton, IL: Crossway, 2003), 37.